THE MAGIC UMBRELLA

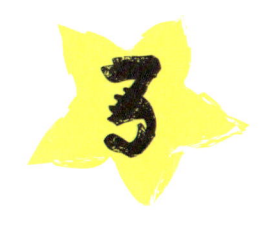

TYRANNOSAURUS, BRATASARUS AND THE Elephant

3

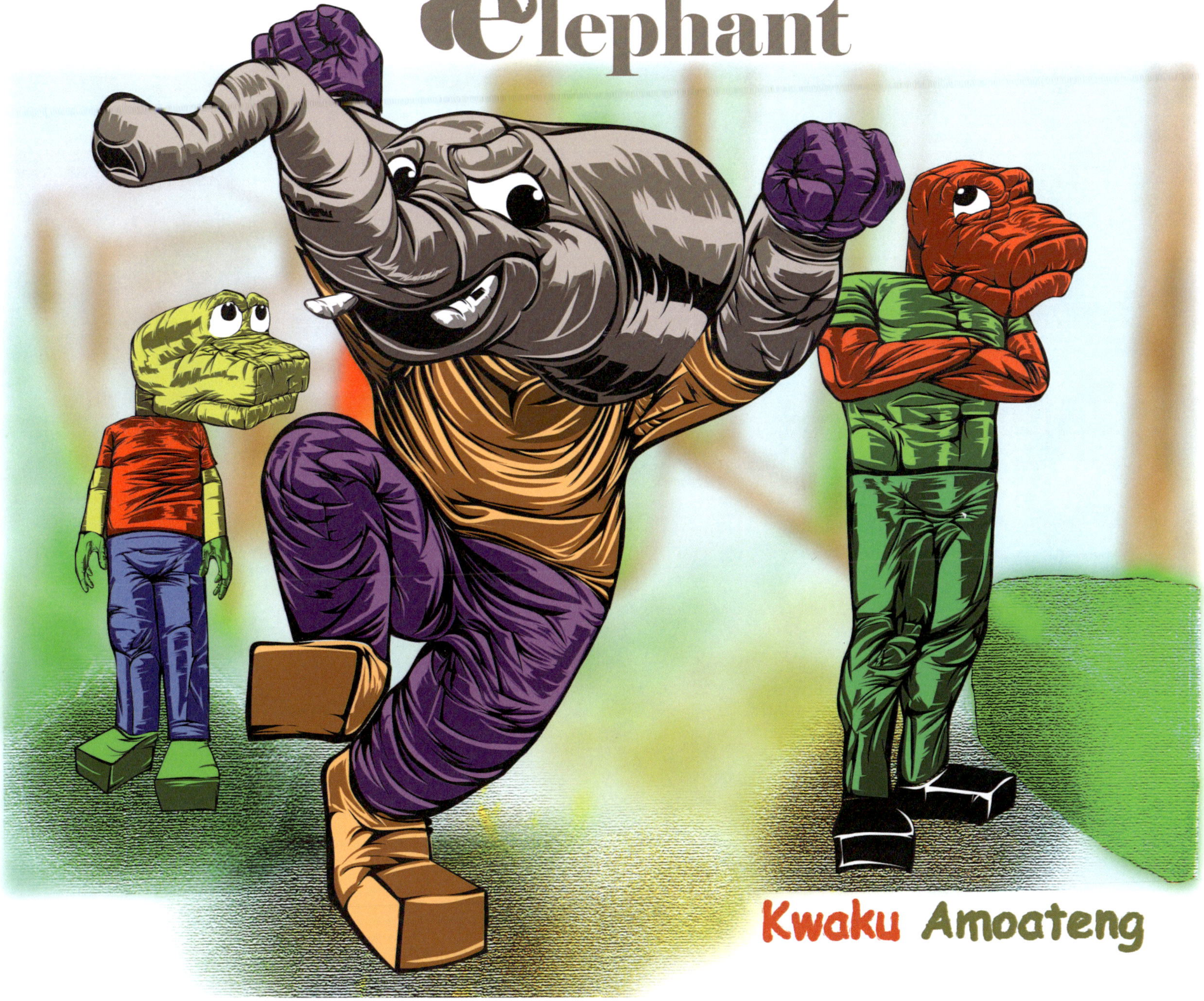

Kwaku Amoateng

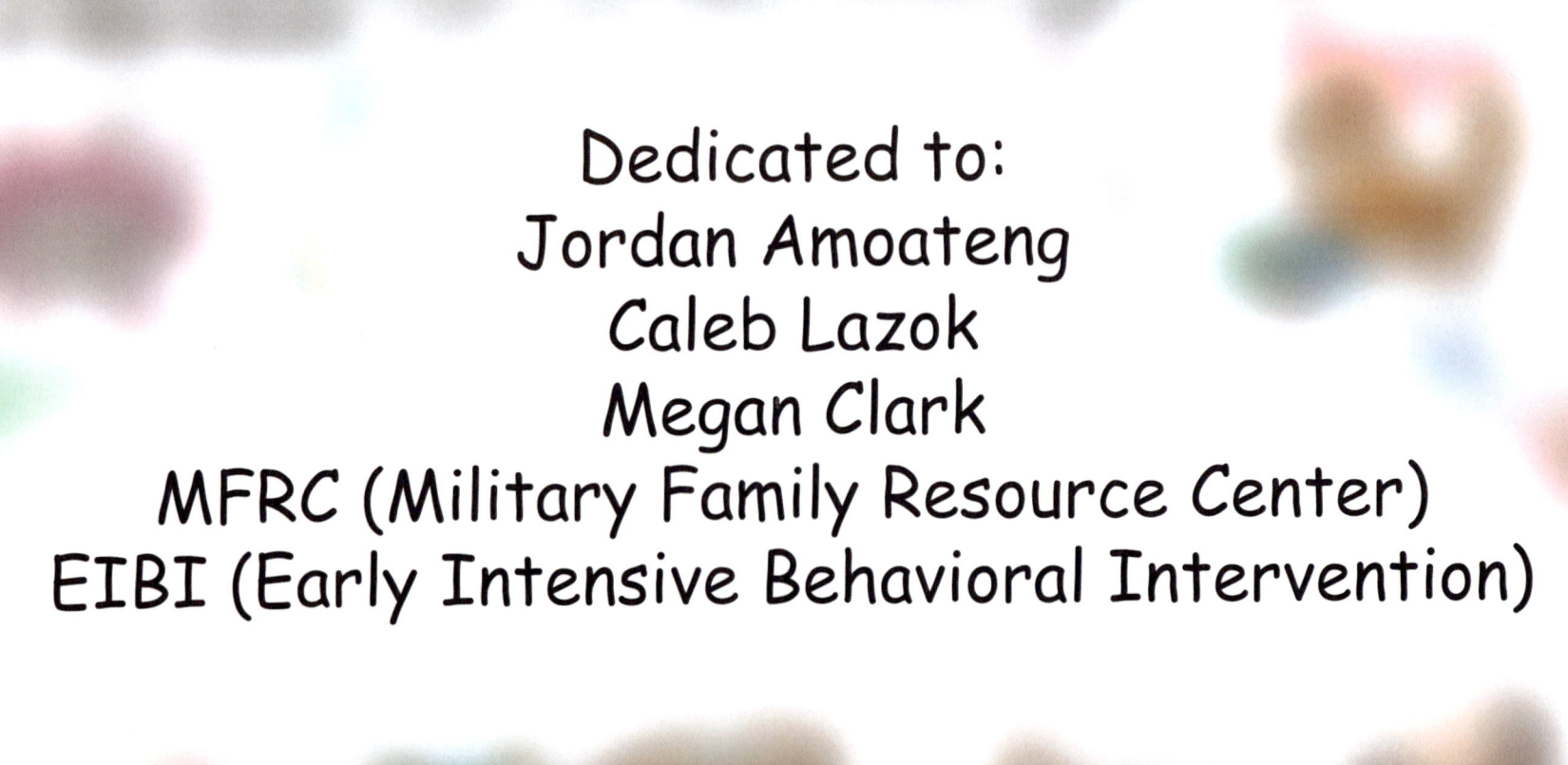

Dedicated to:
Jordan Amoateng
Caleb Lazok
Megan Clark
MFRC (Military Family Resource Center)
EIBI (Early Intensive Behavioral Intervention)

Kwadan and Jorku try to ignore the elephant. This upsets the elephant; he wants Kwadan and Jorku to pay attention to him, so he becomes very noisy and disruptive.

Kwadan and Jorku say goodbye to Jimmy and take to the sky with their magic umbrella. Where do you think they are heading to next?

My name is Kwaku Amoateng and I am the first born of six brothers. I am of Ghanaian Decent, born in Lagos Nigeria. My brothers and I moved to Canada during the early 90s. My beautiful child Jordan, is the most talented kid I know. We both love going on adventures and best of all, we love sharing our adventures.

www.ingramcontent.com/pod-product-compliance
Lightning Source LLC
Chambersburg PA
CBRC101245160426
43209CB00025B/1895